Mountain
of Presidents

Dona Herweck Rice

Publishing Credits

Rachelle Cracchiolo, M.S.Ed., *Publisher*
Conni Medina, M.A.Ed., *Managing Editor*
Jamey Acosta, *Content Director*
Dona Herweck Rice, *Series Developer*
Robin Erickson, *Multimedia Designer*

Image Credits: Cover, p.1 ©iStock.com/blackestockphoto; pp.3-4, 12 (top) ©Underwood &
Underwood/Corbis; p.5 ©iStock.com/JOE CICAK (upper left), ©iStock.com/GeorgiosArt (upper
right); p.5 Library of Congress [LC-DIG-ppmsca-36082]; p.6 ©Everett Collection Historical/Alamy; p.7
©Bettmann/Corbis; pp.8-9 National Park Service; all other images from Shutterstock.

Library of Congress Cataloging-in-Publication Data

Library of Congress Control Number: 2015938709

Teacher Created Materials

5301 Oceanus Drive
Huntington Beach, CA 92649-1030
http://www.tcmpub.com

ISBN 978-1-4938-2057-3

© 2016 Teacher Created Materials, Inc.

Words to Know

carve

Mount
Rushmore

presidents